POWERED UP!

A STEM Approach to Energy Sources

BIOMASS ENERGY

Harnessing the Power of Organic Matter

ELIZABETH KRAJNIK

PowerKiDS press

New York

Published in 2018 by The Rosen Publishing Group, Inc.
29 East 21st Street, New York, NY 10010

First Edition

Editor: Melissa Raé Shofner
Book Design: Tanya Dellaccio

Photo Credits: Cover Ted Horowitz/Alamy Stock Photo; p. 4 (solar panels) pisaphotography/Shuttertock.com; p. 4 (wind turbines) Mimadeo/Shutterstock.com; p. 5 Sean Gallup/Getty Images News/Getty Images; p. 7 MYCHELE DANIAU/AFP/ Getty Images; p. 8 John And Penny/Shutterstock.com; p. 9 (sugarcane) jeep2499/ Shutterstock.com; p. 9 (corn) Songsak P/Shutterstock.com; p. 9 (rapeseed) Aleksandar Dickov/Shutterstock.com; p. 11 (Henry Ford) Keystone/Hulton Archive/Getty Images; p. 11 (Model T) Three Lions/Hulton Archive/Getty Images; p. 13 Jerry Redfern/ LightRocket/Getty Images; p. 14 (both) DANIEL HAYDUK/AFP/Getty Images; p. 15 Filimages/Shutterstock.com; p. 17 (both) Jim West/imageBROKER/Getty Images; p. 18 Alzbeta/Shutterstock.com; p. 19 (recycling center) JONATHAN NACKSTRAND/ AFP/Getty Images; p. 19 (traffic jam) blvdone/Shutterstock.com; p. 21 Scott Sinklier/ Passage/Getty Images; p. 22 MarekPiotrowski/Shutterstock.com.

Library of Congress Cataloging-in-Publication Data

Names: Krajnik, Elizabeth, author.
Title: Biomass energy : harnessing the power of organic matter / Elizabeth Krajnik.
Description: New York : PowerKids Press, [2018] | Series: Powered up! : a STEM approach to energy sources | Includes bibliographical references and index.
Identifiers: LCCN 2017019046| ISBN 9781538328507 (pbk. book) | ISBN 9781508164296 (library bound book) | ISBN 9781538328569 (6 pack)
Subjects: LCSH: Biomass energy–Juvenile literature.
Classification: LCC TP339 .K73 2018 | DDC 662/.88–dc23
LC record available at https://lccn.loc.gov/2017019046

Manufactured in China

CPSIA Compliance Information: Batch #BW18PK For Further Information contact Rosen Publishing, New York, New York at 1-800-237-9932

CONTENTS

ALTERNATIVE ENERGY NOW

In 1950, there were about 2.5 billion people living on Earth. In 2005, the population reached 6.5 billion people. Scientists believe there could be more than 9 billion people on our planet by 2050.

As the world's population increases, so does the amount of energy used each day. Unfortunately, the fossil fuels we often depend on for energy are harming the **environment**. They're also running out. Today, scientists are exploring how **alternative** energy sources can power Earth into the future.

WIND POWER

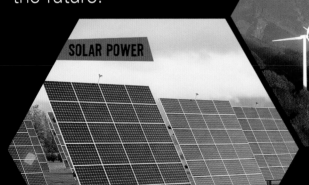

SOLAR POWER

FOSSIL FUELS, SUCH AS OIL, NATURAL GAS, AND COAL, FORM INSIDE THE EARTH FROM ANIMALS AND PLANTS THAT DIED MILLIONS OF YEARS AGO. BURNING THEM PRODUCES ENERGY BUT ALSO CREATES A LOT OF POLLUTION.

SUPERCHARGED!

Alternative energy sources are renewable and better for the environment than fossil fuels. Solar power, wind power, and biomass are examples of alternative energy sources.

WHAT IS BIOMASS?

Biomass is plant matter and animal waste that can be used as fuel. Forms of biomass have been used as energy sources for thousands of years.

Plants create their own food through photosynthesis. This is when plants take in carbon dioxide, water, and sunlight and create energy (in the form of sugars) and oxygen. When an animal eats plants, some of this energy is **transferred** to its waste. When biomass is burned, the energy stored inside the plant matter is released, or let go.

SUPERCHARGED!

Biomass is a low-cost energy source. Plants and animal waste can be easily found in nature, making biomass readily available.

SOME FARMS IN THE UNITED STATES HAVE STARTED USING COW WASTE, CALLED MANURE, AS A FUEL SOURCE. THIS "COW POWER" OFTEN PROVIDES ENOUGH ENERGY TO RUN THE FARMS AND SOMETIMES THE SURROUNDING TOWNS, TOO!

COMMON SOURCES OF BIOMASS

Three big sources of biomass are forests, waste **materials**, and farms. There are two types of biomass materials: woody and nonwoody. Woody biomass materials from forests include logs and bark chips. Some farms grow special types of trees that are used as biomass. Waste from trees, such as sawdust, is also a source of woody biomass.

Nonwoody sources of biomass include grains, grasses, and oils that come from crops. Waste oils, waste fats, and gases from **landfills** make up a significant source of nonwoody biomass.

PEAT BLOCKS

SUGARCANE

CORN

SUPERCHARGED!

Some of the most common nonwoody sources of biomass are sugarcane, corn, and rapeseed. These plants are used to make **biofuels** such as ethanol and biodiesel.

RAPESEED

◄ PARTLY DECOMPOSED, OR ROTTEN, PLANT MATTER CALLED PEAT IS SOMETIMES COLLECTED AND USED AS FUEL.

EARLY BIOMASS

Long ago, people discovered fire and learned to burn biomass as a source of heat. Wood was an important fuel source. Today, many people still burn biomass to heat their homes.

During the 1800s, society began to focus more on industry, or making things with machines and factories. Around this time, people discovered ways to use biomass energy on a larger scale. Biofuels such as ethanol have been an important source of energy for over a century.

SUPERCHARGED!

Today, most of the gasoline used as fuel in the United States is mixed with ethanol. Some gasoline contains 10 percent ethanol, while other kinds contain 15 percent or more ethanol.

HENRY FORD

HENRY FORD BELIEVED ETHANOL WOULD BE THE FUEL OF THE FUTURE. HE DESIGNED THE EARLIEST MODEL T AUTOMOBILES SO THEY COULD RUN ON ETHANOL AS WELL AS PETROLEUM, WHICH IS A POPULAR TYPE OF FOSSIL FUEL.

MODEL T FORD

11

BIOMASS CONSUMERS

Countries around the world use biomass to produce energy. Many of the countries that burn the most biomass are in Africa. In these countries, up to 90 percent of people get their energy in this way.

Some of these countries depend heavily on biomass because they don't have as much access to other energy sources. In Western countries, such as the United States, most people use electricity or natural gas to heat their homes and cook their food.

SUPERCHARGED!

Biomass wasn't an official term until the 1970s. It was around this time that scientists became interested in developing biomass on a large scale as an alternative to fossil fuels.

WOOD AND OTHER FORMS OF BIOMASS CAN PRODUCE MORE SMOKE THAN THEY DO HEAT. COOKING INSIDE OVER AN OPEN FIRE MAY CAUSE HEALTH PROBLEMS.

USING BIOMASS

Biomass can be used to generate, or create, heat, electricity, and biofuel. First, the biomass must be dried, which reduces its size but keeps almost all its energy. The drying **process** is called torrefaction.

To use biomass to create electricity, small blocks of dried biomass called briquettes are burned to produce steam. The steam powers a **turbine** that turns a machine called a generator, which produces electricity. This process is known as direct firing. Biomass and coal are often burned together, which is known as cofiring.

PACKAGED BRIQUETTES

CHICKEN MANURE CAN BE USED TO CREATE ELECTRICITY. A PROCESS KNOWN AS GASIFICATION SEPARATES THE GASES IN CHICKEN MANURE FROM THE SOLID WASTE. THE GAS IS THEN BURNED TO GENERATE ELECTRICITY.

SUPERCHARGED!

Cofiring biomass and coal reduces the amount of coal we burn, which reduces the **greenhouse gases** released. Also, separate factories don't need to be built for burning biomass alone.

LANDFILLS CREATE BIOGAS

Most of our household trash is taken to landfills. This waste sits and rots, producing what are known as biogases. One of these gases is methane. Methane can be very dangerous, or unsafe. It may cause fires and explosions.

Methane can be collected from landfills and converted, or changed, into energy. In states where there are many landfills, such as California, producing electricity from methane is a good way to make use of something that could otherwise be harmful.

SUPERCHARGED!

Methane from cow manure can also be used to generate electricity. It's also used to create a fuel called biomethane and renewable natural gas that's used to heat homes.

SMITH CREEK LANDFILL, MICHIGAN

AS OF 2017, THERE ARE 43 LANDFILLS IN MICHIGAN WHERE METHANE GAS IS COLLECTED AND CONVERTED INTO ENERGY. MICHIGAN'S EFFORTS ARE SECOND ONLY TO CALIFORNIA, WHICH COLLECTS AND CONVERTS METHANE AT 81 LANDFILLS.

RECYCLE YOUR HOUSEHOLD WASTE

Each day, the average American throws away about 5 pounds (2.3 kg) of trash that ends up in landfills. While methane gas from landfills can be used as a source of energy, reducing and recycling our household waste is even better.

In Sweden, only about 1 percent of household waste ends up in landfills. Swedish people **compost** their food waste and take other trash to recycling centers. About 50 percent of Sweden's household waste is burned to produce energy.

COMPOST BIN

RECYCLING CENTER, SWEDEN

SUPERCHARGED!

In 2014, Sweden imported, or brought in, about 3 tons (2.7 mt) of waste from other countries to convert into energy.

COMPOSTING FOOD WASTE IS A GOOD WAY TO REDUCE THE AMOUNT OF TRASH IN LANDFILLS AND THE PRODUCTION OF GREENHOUSE GASES. IF AMERICANS COMPOSTED ALL THEIR FOOD WASTE, IT WOULD BE EQUAL TO TAKING 2 MILLION CARS OFF THE ROAD.

DISADVANTAGES OF BIOMASS

Biomass is partly a renewable energy source. People and animals produce solid waste every day, and new trees can be planted. However, biomass isn't renewable in the same way solar and wind power are.

If humans depend too much on biomass for creating energy, they could harm the environment. Forests need healthy soil, and trees take a long time to grow.

Burning biomass produces harmful chemicals, which can pollute the air we breathe. Some studies show that burning biomass may create more pollutants than burning fossil fuels.

SUPERCHARGED!

Biomass is not a completely **sustainable** source of energy. Unfortunately, most biomass factories still need fossil fuels to operate.

HARVESTING, OR COLLECTING, CROPS FOR BIOMASS USES
FOSSIL FUELS. THESE CROPS MUST THEN BE TRANSPORTED TO
A PROCESSING PLANT, WHICH ALSO REQUIRES FOSSIL FUELS.

THE FUTURE OF BIOMASS

Scientists and **engineers** hold the future of biomass in their hands. They're working hard to find ways to make using biomass for energy more sustainable. They hope to increase the amount of energy biomass produces and decrease the amount of fossil fuels used throughout the process.

Biomass can be a less expensive way to provide people with important things such as heat and electricity. Today, biomass supplies about 14 percent of the world's energy. It's one of the energy sources of the future!

BIOMASS POWER PLANT, POLAND

GLOSSARY

alternative: Something that can be chosen instead of something else.

biofuel: A fuel made of or produced from matter that was once living.

compost: The process of turning plant material into a product that makes soil richer.

engineer: Someone who uses math and science to do useful things, such as build machines.

environment: The conditions that surround a living thing and affect the way it lives.

greenhouse gases: Gases in the atmosphere that trap energy from the sun.

landfill: A place where waste is buried between layers of earth.

material: Something from which something else can be made.

process: A set of actions that lead to a particular result.

sustainable: Able to last a long time.

transfer: To move or carry from one person, place, or thing to another.

turbine: An engine with blades that are caused to spin by pressure from water, steam, or air.

INDEX

WEBSITES

Due to the changing nature of Internet links, PowerKids Press has developed an online list of websites related to the subject of this book. This site is updated regularly. Please use this link to access the list: www.powerkidslinks.com/pu/bio